PIANO | VOCAL | GUITAR ▪ CD   **VOLUME 114**

HAL•LEONARD

PIANO PLAY-ALONG

MOTOWN

T0087151

ISBN 978-1-4584-0649-1

HAL•LEONARD®
CORPORATION

7777 W. BLUEMOUND RD. P.O. BOX 13819 MILWAUKEE, WI 53213

In Australia Contact:
Hal Leonard Australia Pty. Ltd.
4 Lentara Court
Cheltenham, Victoria, 3192 Australia
Email: ausadmin@halleonard.com.au

For all works contained herein:
Unauthorized copying, arranging, adapting, recording, Internet posting, public performance,
or other distribution of the printed or recorded music in this publication is an infringement of copyright.
Infringers are liable under the law.

Visit Hal Leonard Online at
www.halleonard.com

CONTENTS

AIN'T NO MOUNTAIN HIGH ENOUGH

Words and Music by NICKOLAS ASHFORD
and VALERIE SIMPSON

With a steady beat

Now, if you need me, call ____ me. No mat-ter where you
I set you free? _____ I told you you could

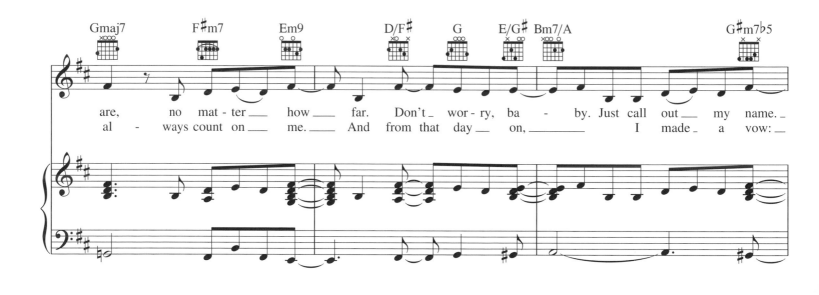

are, no mat-ter ___ how ___ far. Don't wor-ry, ba - by. Just call out ___ my name. ___
al - ways count on ___ me. ___ And from that day ___ on, _____ I made ___ a vow: ___

____ I'll be there in a hur - ry. ___ You don't have to wor - ry, 'cause, ba-by, there
____ I'll be there when you want ___ me, ___ some way, ___ some - how. _____ 'Cause, ba - by, there

© 1967, 1970 (Renewed 1995, 1998) JOBETE MUSIC CO., INC.
All Rights Controlled and Administered by EMI APRIL MUSIC INC.
All Rights Reserved   International Copyright Secured   Used by Permission

I CAN'T HELP MYSELF
(Sugar Pie, Honey Bunch)

Words and Music by BRIAN HOLLAND,
LAMONT DOZIER and EDWARD HOLLAND

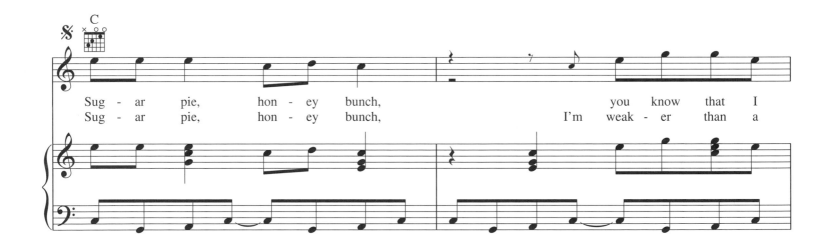

© 1965, 1972 (Renewed 1993, 2000) JOBETE MUSIC CO., INC.
All Rights Controlled and Administered by EMI BLACKWOOD MUSIC INC. on behalf of STONE AGATE MUSIC (A Division of JOBETE MUSIC CO., INC.)
All Rights Reserved   International Copyright Secured   Used by Permission

LET'S GET IT ON

Words and Music by MARVIN GAYE
and ED TOWNSEND

Slow Soul beat

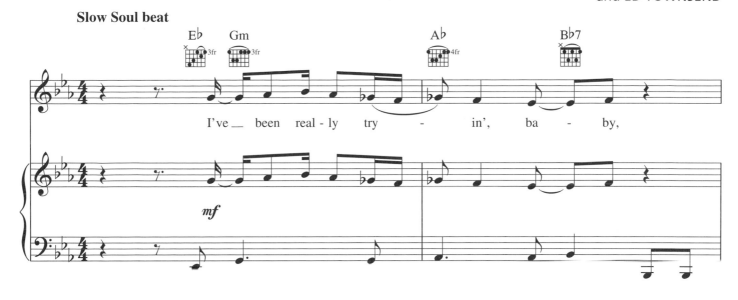

I've __ been real - ly try - in', ba - by,

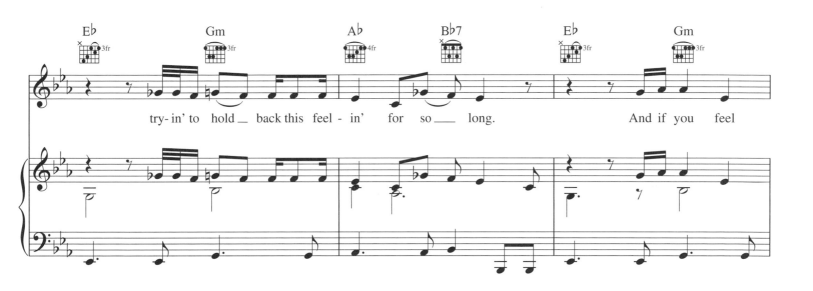

try - in' to hold __ back this feel - in' for so __ long. And if you feel

like __ I feel, __ ba - by, then come on, __ on, __ come on. Ooh, __ let's get it

© 1973 (Renewed 2001) JOBETE MUSIC CO., INC. and STONE DIAMOND MUSIC CORP.
All Rights Controlled and Administered by EMI APRIL MUSIC INC. and EMI BLACKWOOD MUSIC INC.
All Rights Reserved   International Copyright Secured   Used by Permission

I HEARD IT THROUGH THE GRAPEVINE

Words and Music by NORMAN J. WHITFIELD
and BARRETT STRONG

© 1966 (Renewed 1994) JOBETE MUSIC CO., INC.
All Rights Controlled and Administered by EMI BLACKWOOD MUSIC INC. on behalf of STONE AGATE MUSIC (A Division of JOBETE MUSIC CO., INC.)
All Rights Reserved   International Copyright Secured   Used by Permission

MY GIRL

Words and Music by WILLIAM "SMOKEY" ROBINSON
and RONALD WHITE

© 1964, 1972, 1973, 1977 (Renewed 1992, 2000, 2001, 2005) JOBETE MUSIC CO., INC.
All Rights Controlled and Administered by EMI APRIL MUSIC INC.
All Rights Reserved   International Copyright Secured   Used by Permission

(Talk - in' 'bout my girl, my girl,
e - ven got the month _ of May with my girl. _____

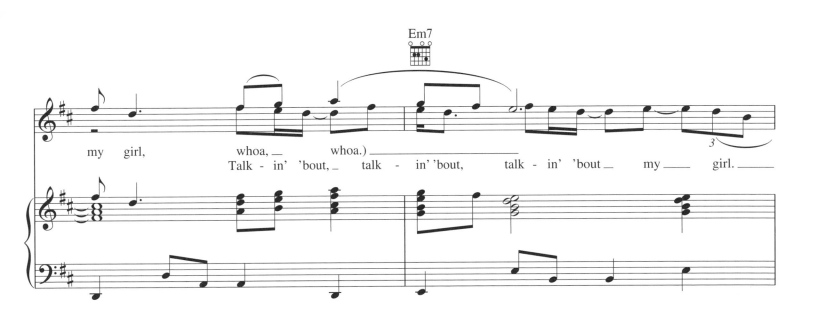

my girl, whoa, __ whoa.) ____
Talk - in' 'bout, _ talk - in' 'bout, talk - in' 'bout _ my ___ girl. ____

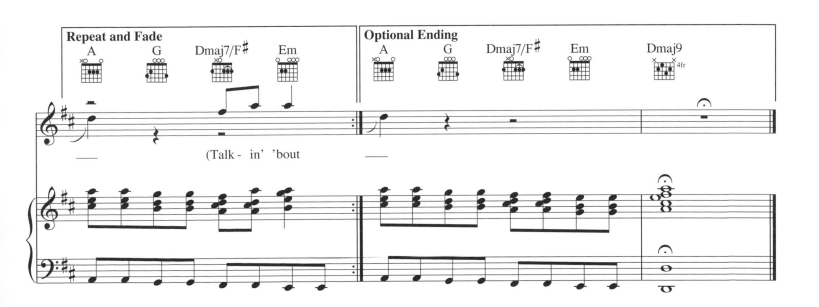

Repeat and Fade

(Talk - in' 'bout

Optional Ending

WHAT'S GOING ON

Words and Music by RENALDO BENSON,
ALFRED CLEVELAND and MARVIN GAYE

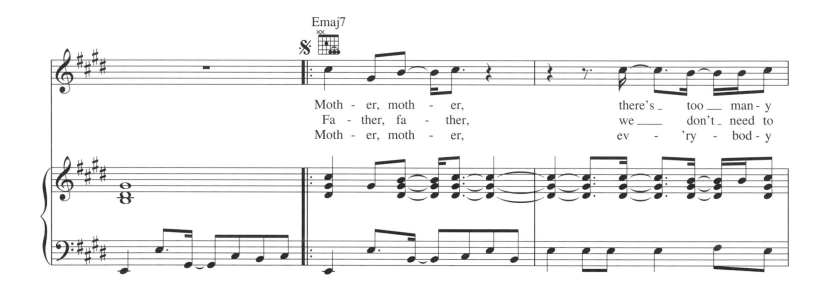

Moth - er, moth - er,   there's_ too_ man - y
Fa - ther, fa - ther,   we_ don't need to
Moth - er, moth - er,   ev - 'ry - bod - y

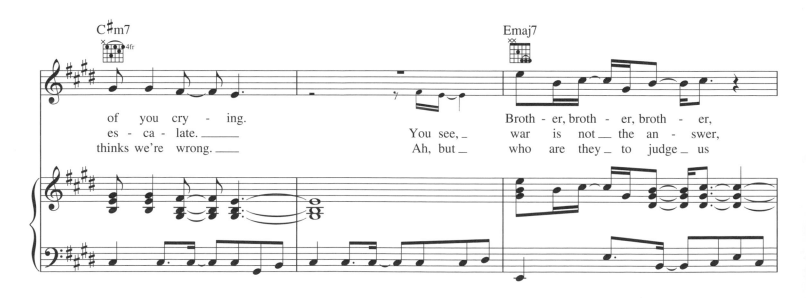

of you cry - ing.   Broth - er, broth - er, broth - er,
es - ca - late.___   You see,_ war is not_ the an - swer,
thinks we're wrong.___   Ah, but_ who are they_ to judge_ us

© 1970 (Renewed 1998) JOBETE MUSIC CO., INC., MGIII MUSIC, NMG MUSIC and FCG MUSIC
All Rights Controlled and Administered by EMI APRIL MUSIC INC. on behalf of JOBETE MUSIC CO., INC.,
MGIII MUSIC, NMG MUSIC and FCG MUSIC and EMI BLACKWOOD MUSIC INC. on behalf of STONE AGATE MUSIC (A Division of JOBETE MUSIC CO., INC.)
All Rights Reserved   International Copyright Secured   Used by Permission

YOU CAN'T HURRY LOVE

Words and Music by EDWARD HOLLAND,
LAMONT DOZIER and BRIAN HOLLAND

© 1965, 1966 (Renewed 1993, 1994) JOBETE MUSIC CO., INC.
All Rights Controlled and Administered by EMI BLACKWOOD MUSIC INC. on behalf of STONE AGATE MUSIC (A Division of JOBETE MUSIC CO., INC.)
All Rights Reserved   International Copyright Secured   Used by Permission

REACH OUT, I'LL BE THERE

Words and Music by BRIAN HOLLAND,
LAMONT DOZIER and EDWARD HOLLAND

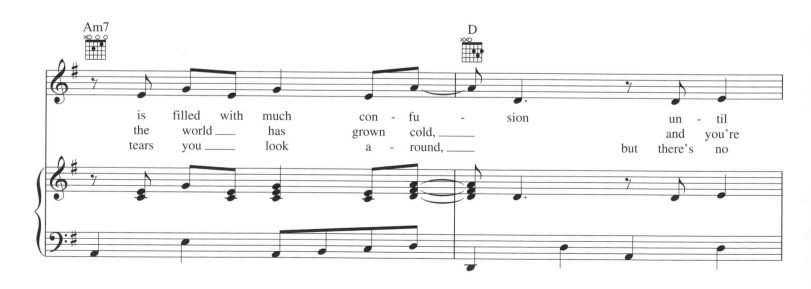

© 1966 (Renewed 1994) JOBETE MUSIC CO., INC.
All Rights Controlled and Administered by EMI BLACKWOOD MUSIC INC. on behalf of STONE AGATE MUSIC (A Division of JOBETE MUSIC CO., INC.)
All Rights Reserved   International Copyright Secured   Used by Permission

THE ULTIMATE SONGBOOKS

HAL•LEONARD

These great songbook/CD packs come with our standard arrangements for piano and voice with guitar chord frames plus a CD.

The CD includes a full performance of each song, as well as a second track without the piano part so you can play "lead" with the band!

PIANO PLAY-ALONG

1. **Movie Music** 00311072 ....$14.95
2. **Jazz Ballads** 00311073 ....$14.95
3. **Timeless Pop** 00311074 ....$14.99
4. **Broadway Classics** 00311075 ....$14.95
5. **Disney** 00311076 ....$14.95
6. **Country Standards** 00311077 ....$14.99
7. **Love Songs** 00311078 ....$14.95
8. **Classical Themes** 00311079 ....$14.95
9. **Children's Songs** 0311080 ....$14.95
10. **Wedding Classics** 00311081 ....$14.95
11. **Wedding Favorites** 00311097 ....$14.95
12. **Christmas Favorites** 00311137 ....$15.95
13. **Yuletide Favorites** 00311138 ....$14.95
14. **Pop Ballads** 00311145 ....$14.95
15. **Favorite Standards** 00311146 ....$14.95
17. **Movie Favorites** 00311148 ....$14.95
18. **Jazz Standards** 00311149 ....$14.95
19. **Contemporary Hits** 00311162 ....$14.95
20. **R&B Ballads** 00311163 ....$14.95
21. **Big Band** 00311164 ....$14.95
22. **Rock Classics** 00311165 ....$14.95
23. **Worship Classics** 00311166 ....$14.95
24. **Les Misérables** 00311169 ....$14.95
25. **The Sound of Music** 00311175 ....$15.99
26. **Andrew Lloyd Webber Favorites** 00311178 ....$14.95
27. **Andrew Lloyd Webber Greats** 00311179 ....$14.95
28. **Lennon & McCartney** 00311180 ....$14.95
29. **The Beach Boys** 00311181 ....$14.95
30. **Elton John** 00311182 ....$14.95
31. **Carpenters** 00311183 ....$14.95
32. **Bacharach & David** 00311218 ....$14.95
33. **Peanuts™** 00311227 ....$14.95
34. **Charlie Brown Christmas** 00311228 ....$15.95
35. **Elvis Presley Hits** 00311230 ....$14.95
36. **Elvis Presley Greats** 00311231 ....$14.95
37. **Contemporary Christian** 00311232 $14.95
38. **Duke Ellington – Standards** 00311233 ....$14.95
39. **Duke Ellington – Classics** 00311234 ....$14.95
40. **Showtunes** 00311237 ....$14.95
41. **Rodgers & Hammerstein** 00311238 $14.95
42. **Irving Berlin** 00311239 ....$14.95
43. **Jerome Kern** 00311240 ....$14.95

44. **Frank Sinatra – Popular Hits** 00311277 ....$14.95
45. **Frank Sinatra – Most Requested Songs** 00311278 ....$14.95
46. **Wicked** 00311317 ....$15.99
47. **Rent** 00311319 ....$14.95
48. **Christmas Carols** 00311332 ....$14.95
49. **Holiday Hits** 00311333 ....$15.99
50. **Disney Classics** 00311417 ....$14.95
51. **High School Musical** 00311421 ....$19.95
52. **Andrew Lloyd Webber Classics** 00311422 ....$14.95
53. **Grease** 00311450 ....$14.95
54. **Broadway Favorites** 00311451 ....$14.95
55. **The 1940s** 00311453 ....$14.95
56. **The 1950s** 00311459 ....$14.95
57. **The 1960s** 00311460 ....$14.99
58. **The 1970s** 00311461 ....$14.99
59. **The 1980s** 00311462 ....$14.99
60. **The 1990s** 00311463 ....$14.99
61. **Billy Joel Favorites** 00311464 ....$14.95
62. **Billy Joel Hits** 00311465 ....$14.95
63. **High School Musical 2** 00311470 .....$19.95
64. **God Bless America** 00311489 ....$14.95
65. **Casting Crowns** 00311494 ....$14.95
66. **Hannah Montana** 00311772 ....$19.95
67. **Broadway Gems** 00311803 ....$14.99
68. **Lennon & McCartney Favorites** 00311804 ....$14.99
69. **Pirates of the Caribbean** 00311807 ....$14.95
70. **"Tomorrow," "Put on a Happy Face," And Other Charles Strouse Hits** 00311821 ....$14.99
71. **Rock Band** 00311822 ....$14.99
72. **High School Musical 3** 00311826 .....$19.99
73. **Mamma Mia! – The Movie** 00311831 ....$14.99
74. **Cole Porter** 00311844 ....$14.99
75. **Twilight** 00311860 ....$16.99
76. **Pride & Prejudice** 00311862 ....$14.99
77. **Elton John Favorites** 00311884 ....$14.99
78. **Eric Clapton** 00311885 ....$14.99
79. **Tangos** 00311886 ....$14.99
80. **Fiddler on the Roof** 00311887 ....$14.99

81. **Josh Groban** 00311901 ....$14.99
82. **Lionel Richie** 00311902 ....$14.99
83. **Phantom of the Opera** 00311903 ....$14.99
84. **Antonio Carlos Jobim Favorites** 00311919 ....$14.99
85. **Latin Favorites** 00311920 ....$14.99
86. **Barry Manilow** 00311935 ....$14.99
87. **Patsy Cline** 00311936 ....$14.99
88. **Neil Diamond** 00311937 ....$14.99
89. **Favorite Hymns** 00311940 ....$14.99
90. **Irish Favorites** 00311969 ....$14.99
91. **Broadway Jazz** 00311972 ....$14.99
92. **Disney Favorites** 00311973 ....$14.99
93. **The Twilight Saga: New Moon – Soundtrack** 00311974 ....$16.99
94. **The Twilight Saga: New Moon – Score** 00311975 ....$16.99
95. **Taylor Swift** 00311984 ....$14.99
96. **Best of Lennon & McCartney** 00311996 ....$14.99
97. **Great Classical Themes** 00312020 . $14.99
98. **Christmas Cheer** 00312021 ....$14.99
99. **Antonio Carlos Jobim Classics** 00312039 ....$14.99
100. **Country Classics** 00312041 ....$14.99
101. **Broadway Hits** 00312042 ....$14.99
102. **Glee** 00312043 ....$14.99
103. **Gospel Favorites** 00312044 ....$14.99
104. **Great Songs** 00312054 ....$19.99
105. **Bee Gees** 00312055 ....$14.99
106. **Carole King** 00312056 ....$14.99
107. **Bob Dylan** 00312057 ....$16.99
108. **Simon & Garfunkel** 00312058 ....$16.99
109. **Top Hits** 00312068 ....$14.99
110. **Henry Mancini** 00312077 ....$14.99
111. **Stevie Wonder** 00312119 ....$14.99

FOR MORE INFORMATION, SEE YOUR LOCAL MUSIC DEALER, OR WRITE TO:

HAL•LEONARD® CORPORATION

7777 W. BLUEMOUND RD. P.O. BOX 13819 MILWAUKEE, WI 53213

Visit Hal Leonard Online at **www.halleonard.com**

Prices, contents, and availability subject to change without notice.

0311

Big Books of Music

Our "Big Books" feature big selections of popular titles under one cover, perfect for performing musicians, music aficionados or the serious hobbyist. All books are arranged for piano, voice, and guitar, and feature stay-open binding, so the books lie flat without breaking the spine.

BIG BOOK OF BALLADS – 2ND ED.
62 songs.
00310485 ....$19.95

BIG BOOK OF BIG BAND HITS
84 songs.
00310701 ....$22.99

BIG BOOK OF BLUEGRASS SONGS
70 songs.
00311484 ....$19.95

BIG BOOK OF BLUES
80 songs.
00311843 ....$19.99

BIG BOOK OF BROADWAY
70 songs.
00311658 ....$19.95

BIG BOOK OF CHILDREN'S SONGS
55 songs.
00359261 ....$16.99

GREAT BIG BOOK OF CHILDREN'S SONGS
76 songs.
00310002 ....$14.95

FANTASTIC BIG BOOK OF CHILDREN'S SONGS
66 songs.
00311062 ....$17.95

MIGHTY BIG BOOK OF CHILDREN'S SONGS
65 songs.
00310467 ....$14.95

REALLY BIG BOOK OF CHILDREN'S SONGS
63 songs.
00310372 ....$17.99

BIG BOOK OF CHILDREN'S MOVIE SONGS
66 songs.
00310731 ....$19.99

BIG BOOK OF CHRISTMAS SONGS – 2ND ED.
126 songs.
00311520 ....$19.95

BIG BOOK OF CLASSIC ROCK
77 songs.
00310801 ....$22.95

BIG BOOK OF CLASSICAL MUSIC
100 songs.
00310508 ....$19.99

BIG BOOK OF CONTEMPORARY CHRISTIAN FAVORITES – 3RD ED.
50 songs.
00312067 ....$21.99

BIG BOOK OF COUNTRY MUSIC – 2ND ED.
63 songs.
00310188 ....$19.95

BIG BOOK OF COUNTRY ROCK
64 songs.
00311748 ....$19.99

BIG BOOK OF EARLY ROCK N' ROLL
99 songs.
00310398 ....$19.95

BIG BOOK OF '50S & '60S SWINGING SONGS
67 songs.
00310982 ....$19.95

BIG BOOK OF FOLK POP ROCK
79 songs.
00311125 ....$24.95

BIG BOOK OF FRENCH SONGS
70 songs.
00311154 ....$19.95

BIG BOOK OF GERMAN SONGS
78 songs.
00311816 ....$19.99

BIG BOOK OF GOSPEL SONGS
100 songs.
00310604 ....$19.95

BIG BOOK OF HYMNS
125 hymns.
00310510 ....$17.95

BIG BOOK OF IRISH SONGS
76 songs.
00310981 ....$19.95

BIG BOOK OF ITALIAN FAVORITES
80 songs.
00311185 ....$19.99

BIG BOOK OF JAZZ – 2ND ED.
75 songs.
00311557 ....$19.95

BIG BOOK OF LATIN AMERICAN SONGS
89 songs.
00311562 ....$19.95

BIG BOOK OF LOVE SONGS
80 songs.
00310784 ....$19.95

BIG BOOK OF MOTOWN
84 songs.
00311061 ....$19.95

BIG BOOK OF MOVIE MUSIC
72 songs.
00311582 ....$19.95

BIG BOOK OF NOSTALGIA
158 songs.
00310004 ....$24.99

BIG BOOK OF OLDIES
73 songs.
00310756 ....$19.95

BIG BOOK OF RAGTIME PIANO
63 songs.
00311749 ....$19.95

BIG BOOK OF RHYTHM & BLUES
67 songs.
00310169 ....$19.95

BIG BOOK OF ROCK
78 songs.
00311566 ....$22.95

BIG BOOK OF ROCK BALLADS
67 songs.
00311839 ....$22.99

BIG BOOK OF SOUL
71 songs.
00310771 ....$19.95

BIG BOOK OF STANDARDS
86 songs.
00311667 ....$19.95

BIG BOOK OF SWING
84 songs.
00310359 ....$19.95

BIG BOOK OF TORCH SONGS – 2ND ED.
75 songs.
00310561 ....$19.99

BIG BOOK OF TV THEME SONGS
78 songs.
00310504 ....$19.95

BIG BOOK OF WEDDING MUSIC
77 songs.
00311567 ....$19.95

FOR MORE INFORMATION, SEE YOUR LOCAL MUSIC DEALER, OR WRITE TO:

HAL•LEONARD® CORPORATION

7777 W. BLUEMOUND RD. P.O. BOX 13819 MILWAUKEE, WI 53213

Prices, contents, and availability subject to change without notice.

Visit **www.halleonard.com**
for our entire catalog and to view our complete songlists.